5 Secrets of Goal Setting Workbook

Documenting your Action Plan for getting the most from life

by
Dwayne Baptist

志 *Press*

5 Secrets of Goal Setting Workbook

Documenting your Action Plan for getting the most from life

by
Dwayne Baptist

志 *Press*

Published by Kokorozashi Press
Fredericksburg, VA
For more information, visit
5SecretsOfGoalSetting.com
Or send email to: info@5SecretsOfGoalSetting.com

5 Secrets of Goal Setting Workbook

Table of Contents

Welcome to the
5 Secrets of Goal Setting Workbook

Are you ready to have more? To get more? To be more? The fact that you have purchased this workbook indicates to me that you are serious about making the coming year your best ever.

If you have read *5 Secrets of Goal Setting*, the companion to this workbook, then you are probably already familiar with this simple success formula:

- Decide what you really want
- Create a burning desire to have it
- Make a plan, so that you know how to get there
- Carry it out with enthusiasm and abandon

In *5 Secrets of Goal Setting* I go into great depth explaining the theory behind this formula using the following acrostic:

G: **Getting Great Goals**

O: **Overcoming You**

A: **Achieving Alignment**

L: **Learning and Adjusting**

S: **Staying the Course**

5 Secrets of Goal Setting and this workbook are organized into five sections based on GOALS. Let us examine what we will explore in each part.

5 Secrets of Goal Setting Workbook

G: Getting Great Goals

You must know what you want and develop a burning desire in order to achieve your goals. *5 Secrets of Goal Setting* explains how to set SMART goals – Specific, Measurable, Achievable, Relevant, and Timely – and explains the power of the 5-Step Goal Setting Process. This workbook leads you through the 5-Step process for setting and achieving your goals. The process will help you get clear about what it is you are going to do and create a burning desire to achieve your goals.

O: Overcoming You

You must tame the two-headed monster, Fear and Procrastination, in order to keep moving and achieve your goals. *5 Secrets of Goal Setting* discusses numerous strategies for dealing with procrastination and fear when you encounter them. This workbook provides two exercises that will help you proactively fight fear and procrastination. The first helps you identify and eliminate major distractions you are tolerating that sap your time and energy. The second exercise shows you the power of gratitude to overcome fear and make your life more productive.

A: Achieving Alignment

You must focus on the things that are truly important to you in order to maximize your activity and achieve your goals. *5 Secrets of Goal Setting* explains how your value system and your ambitions—the really big things you want to accomplish with your life—can serve as the stars and map to help you navigate life. This workbook takes you through an exercise to define your most important values. Next, you will explore your ambitions though a guided exercise.

L: Learning and Adjusting

You must check your progress to make sure you are heading towards your goals and making the changes you need to get where you want to be. *5 Secrets of Goal Setting* discusses how to conduct regular reviews and to gather and use the lessons you learn along the way. This workbook shares daily, weekly, and monthly review routines that ensure you stay on track with your goals.

S: Staying the Course

You must stay the course and keep taking Focused Action in order to achieve your goals. *5 Secrets of Goal Setting* discusses the need to smell the roses along the way and to turn problems into opportunities. This workbook gives you an exercise to get you moving when stuck.

As You Get Started

The key to achieving your goals is FOCUSED ACTION. There is no substitute for it. Do not fool yourself into believing that you will learn the concepts simply by reading though the workbook. You will become *aware* of the principles by reading, but you will not really *learn* them merely reading. Awareness is important because we cannot begin to understand or explore something if we are not aware of it. For example, mankind did not begin to win regularly in the battle against disease until we became aware of germs and viruses. Only then could we begin to isolate the causes of diseases and begin the experimentation process required to conquer them.

Much of what we think of as "learning" is the process of becoming aware and understanding a subject. As with scientists, the way we really learn something is to take action. In fact, we must take enough action that we master the subject. This workbook is a tool to help you master goal setting and achievement.

If practice is necessary in order to learn and master something, then all success will naturally involve trial and failure along the way. Remember that falling short on a particular effort no more makes you a failure than completing just one makes you a success. Rather, success only comes from continuing to pursue our goals, even after a particular attempt fails.

Jim Rohn said, "Don't let your learning lead to knowledge. Let it lead to

ACTION." This workbook focuses on helping you do just that by leading you through exercises that employ all of the fundamentals of goal setting and achievement. This book will help you master the fundamentals through application.

Now, let's begin the journey toward achieving your goals!

How to Use This Workbook

The *5 Secrets of Goal Setting Workbook* contains five chapters that correspond to the parts of *5 Secrets of Goal Setting*. Each chapter will have a brief overview of the concepts discussed in the book. Following the overview will be exercises based on the exercises presented in the *5 Secrets of Goal Setting*, adapted and expanded for the workbook.

Each exercise will have instructions and worksheets. At the end of each exercise will be reminders to give you confidence you completed it correctly. Finally, there will be tips to ensure you follow through and continue to apply what you have learned to master the concepts.

If you want to print out additional copies of the individual worksheets, you can find them at http://www.5SecretsOfGoalSetting.com/WorkbookResources. Use the password 5SOGSwb~ to access the page.

Chapter 1

G: Getting Great Goals

"Whatever the mind of man can conceive and believe, it can achieve."
—Napoleon Hill

Overview of Getting Great Goals

Goals are the building blocks of all success in life. Earl Nightingale said, "Success is the progressive realization of a worthwhile goal or objective." The process for achieving your goals is:

- Decide what you really want
- Create a burning desire to have it
- Make a plan, so that you know how to get there
- Carry it out with enthusiasm and abandon

The first three elements create focus and the last element is the action. How do you develop goals that can bring these to focus? The key is to set SMART goals. The diagram below shows the attributes of SMART goals.

The Attributes of S M A R T Goals

Specific	Measurable	Attainable	Relevant	Timely
Detailed	Stepping stones	Believe it's achievable	Aligns with values and priorities	Right time to pursue goal
Clear	Evaluates progress	Ambitious & realistic	To the Purpose	Sufficient time to complete
Explicit	Makes goal real	Clarity	Pertinent	Clear target time frame
Particular outcome	Conveys desired outcome	Viable	Applicable	

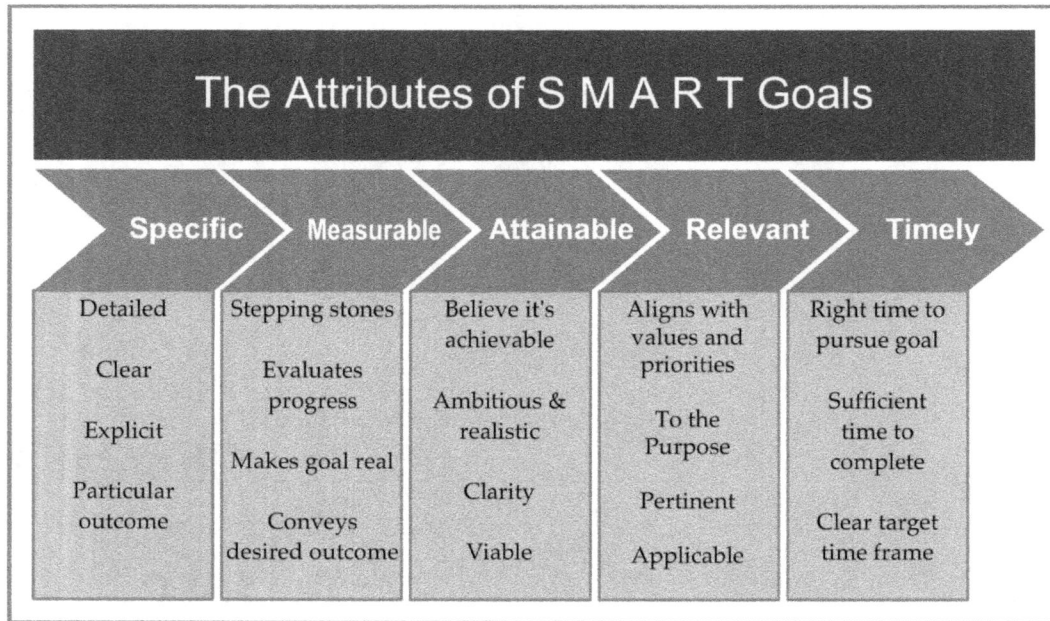

The 5-Step Goal Setting Process embraces SMART and helps you be clear, specific, and detailed about your goals so that you can create a burning desire to complete them. The five steps are:

1. Set a SMART goal.
2. Develop a vision—a picture of the goal, achieved.
3. Decide the price you will pay.
4. Outline your plan.
5. Study your goal daily.

The process gets you to think carefully about what you want and why you want it. Earl Nightingale also said The Strangest Secret in life is that "we become what we think about." Being specific about what you want and why you want it is the first step to building a burning desire. The 5 Step Goal Setting Process documents your goals so that you can keep them in front of you daily. Either you will build a burning desire to achieve your goal or you will abandon it because you realize that you really did not want it. The first will get you what you want. The second will help avoid wasting time and effort toward wrong things.

Since FOCUSED ACTION is the key to achieving goals, it is important that you immediately take action to make your goal real. When you develop your goal, think about something, however small, that you can do that day to begin the journey toward your goal. No, making the plans does not count. You need to do something specific. In *5 Secrets of Goal Setting* I use the example of climbing Mount Everest in five years. If you have never been mountain climbing, then finding a climbing gym and signing up for rock-climbing lessons might be a step you could take immediately.

Taking a small step makes the goal more real, and gives you a small success right away. This builds belief, further building your burning desire.

Exercise: Creating a Goal—The 5-Step Goal Setting Process

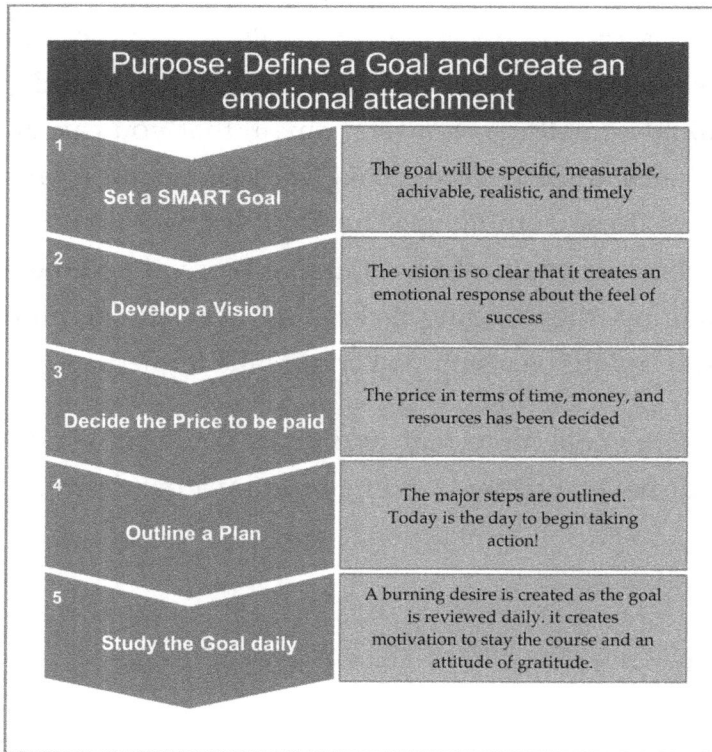

Purpose: Define a Goal and create an emotional attachment

#	Step	Description
1	Set a SMART Goal	The goal will be specific, measurable, achivable, realistic, and timely
2	Develop a Vision	The vision is so clear that it creates an emotional response about the feel of success
3	Decide the Price to be paid	The price in terms of time, money, and resources has been decided
4	Outline a Plan	The major steps are outlined. Today is the day to begin taking action!
5	Study the Goal daily	A burning desire is created as the goal is reviewed daily. it creates motivation to stay the course and an attitude of gratitude.

Are you ready to get clear on your goals and making the strong emotional connection you will need to achieve them? In this exercise, you will learn the 5-Step Goal Setting Process by developing a goal. The worksheet on page 11 will allow you to keep your goal in front of you. You can copy it to something that will be portable enough to keep with you. While you can use the form right away, you might find it useful to use a scratch pad or whiteboard to gather your thoughts before putting the information into the form.

1. Set a SMART goal: Using the SMART questions to help you, found on page 12, develop a specific, measurable, achievable, relevant, and timely goal. In the first section of the worksheet, write a simple statement of your goal as though you already possess it. Also, write down the target date for achieving your goal in the space provided.

2. Develop a vision: As you were applying the SMART process to your goals, you probably thought about who would be involved, what it would be like to achieve the goal, and other details. Develop your clear picture of what the future looks like when you have achieved your goal.

- Describe why you have achieved the goal, your motivation, and how you feel because you have accomplished it.
- Write the vision from the point of view of the person who has just completed the goal. The work done to complete it is in the past. The benefits are now.

3. Decide the price to be paid: Your goal will require sacrifices to achieve. The obvious ones are time and money. Nevertheless, you will have to change, too. Often this is the most challenging price to pay. Determine what you are willing to do to make your goal a reality. This could be something directly related to the goal, such as time, talent, or treasure; it could be a skill you need to acquire or a behavior you need to change.

As an optional part of this step, list the things you are grateful for because you are pursuing this goal. It could be your expected outcome; it might be an aspect of the journey. You can also leave it blank to remind yourself to think about what you are grateful for daily.

4. Outline a plan. Outline the major steps you need to follow in order to achieve your goal. You do not need to have all your steps here, just the major ones that will remind you what to do to stay on track and achieve your goals. You should eventually develop a detailed plan, but you only need the key steps on the 5-Step worksheet in order to remind you and help you build the burning desire in step 5.

Pick something that you can do today in order to start making your goal real. Not planning, but some tangible action that will start the journey. Go do that step now and start making your dream real.

5. Study the goal daily. The 5th step is to keep the worksheet with you and review it daily. Make a point of reading it at least twice daily. Convert it to a form that you can carry it around with you everywhere. I used to do this with 3x5 cards. These days, I take a picture of the form with my iPhone and keep the picture handy wherever I am.

Read the goal sheet aloud at least once a day. If you have written it as though you have achieved it, your subconscious mind will go to work figuring out how to make it happen. Frequently reviewing and vividly imagining your goal achieved will create a burning desire for your goal, helping you to take Focused Action to achieve it.

G: Getting Great Goals

Goal Setting and Achievement Worksheet

Goal	
Target Date	
Vision	
Price	
Gratitude	

Date	Plan Step	Completed

SMART Questions

Keep these questions in mind as you fill in the form on the facing page. They will help you to get the most out of any goal setting activity.

Specific

- What do I want?
- How do I want it?
- When do I want it?
- What are the details of my goal?

Measurable

- How can I measure progress toward my dream?
- In what ways can I quantify my achievements?

Attainable

- What can I do to equip myself for the journey to achieving my goal?
- What resources do I need to get started? To continue to make progress?
- Who do I need to bring with me?

Relevant

- Is this something I really care about?
- Does this goal align with my ambitions?
- How does this fit with my other goals and priorities?

Timely

- What is the timeframe of my goal?
- When must I get started?
- What are the benchmarks for progress and the deadline for completion?

G: Getting Great Goals

Did you remember to...

- Be grateful?
- Pick a price to pay you could really commit to?
  - That price can be a change of habits, acquiring skills, or some other non-money price.
- Review the SMART questions as you set your goal?
- Take an immediate action towards achieving your goal?

Tips for Follow Through

- The secret to achieving your goals is to be very clear about what you want and why you want it, and then keep that information constantly in front of you until you achieve your goal.
- When you create an emotional connection with your goals and act on them, you unleash an unstoppable force.
- Read your goal sheet at least twice daily.
- Keep your goal sheets with you. I take a picture of mine so that I can pull it up on my iPhone whenever I want to read it. Most smartphones have high resolution cameras, making it easy to keep the detail.
- Make sure that you are taking some activity to stay engaged with your goal every day, even if some days it is just something small.

Chapter 2

O: Overcoming You

"When you're worried, and you can't sleep, just count your blessings instead of sheep."
—Irving Berlin, *"Counting Your Blessings"* from White Christmas

Overview of Overcoming You

The number one challenge you face on your success journey is you. As discussed in the previous chapter, you must develop a burning desire to achieve your goals and follow through with Focused Action. Life is going to challenge you with problems and distractions along the way, which can lead to fear and procrastination without that burning desire. Nevertheless, even with a burning desire, we all must deal with those distractions and fears along the way. How do you do that? Let us look at procrastination first; then we will tackle fear.

Pondering Procrastination. Procrastination is doing something other than the thing you said was most important now. Internet entrepreneur and venture capitalist Paul Graham says that some of his most productive friends are the worst procrastinators he knows. He also points out that we procrastinate three different ways:

- Doing nothing instead of what we should be doing.
- Doing something less important than what we should be doing.
- Doing something more important than what we should be doing.

Yes, you can procrastinate doing more important things. The question really is what is the best use of your time at that moment? Paying bills may be less important than finding a cure for cancer, but sometimes it is the best use of your time so that you continue to enjoy a place to live, running water, and electricity. When you think you are procrastinating, you need to confront the situation and handle it. Here is a four-step process for handling procrastination:

1. **Determine if you *are* procrastinating.** If you are procrastinating, acknowledge it. This will force you to confront your actions. If you are stuck rather than procrastinating, check out the exercise in Chapter 5 to get unstuck.

2. **Determine what is important to you now.** As you will see in Chapter 3, our priorities are the result of the trade-offs that must be made so that we can get what we really want. Confirm your priorities and act on them.

3. **Decide how to handle the moment.** There are effective ways to handle procrastination including:

   o *Take a break* – Tired? A deliberate time out to recharge could be just the ticket to get back to work with vigor – and without guilt.
   o *Focus on Your Ambitions and Values* – Are you only focused on the problems rather than the benefits of your ambitions? Relink to the fun and you can get moving again.

- *Take Baby Steps* – Overwhelmed by a job? Break it into smaller pieces and you might get moving again.
- *Change your routine* – Is boredom the real culprit? Switch things up and find new energy.
- *Reward yourself* – Is this bribery? Yes. But finding a small reward for getting through something could be just the incentive you need to keep moving.

4. **Decide how to avoid this situation in the future.** Some distractions are one-off situations while others are chronic affairs. If you are repeating procrastinating behavior, you must address the underlying need. Thomas Leonard, one of the founders of the life coaching movement, calls these unmet needs *Tolerations* because we tolerate them rather than address them. However, failing to address our Tolerations leads to procrastination and frustration paid with time and energy.

Tackling Tolerations. Tolerations are resolved by addressing the underlying need. You can resolve some needs by addressing some environmental aspect. For example, suppose you do not like going to bed at night. One reason for this could be because your bedroom is uninviting: the bed is unmade and clothes are thrown about. Creating the habit of making your bed as soon as you get up and buying a hamper for your clothes could solve the problem. This is an "Environmental" fix for the Toleration.

If, on the other hand, you do not go to bed because you are afraid you will miss something important, you will have to examine your underlying attitudes about what is important and whether those things are likely to require your attention late at night. If you are going to school in the evenings, the late hours might be worth it if you believe the degree is going to lead to a large promotion. The late nights are temporary and you will soon be able to get more sleep. Come to peace with that decision and remind yourself of the good things down the road when you are tempted to fret.

On the other hand, if you are obsessed with politics and feel you MUST know what is in the 15th blog you read daily, you have to ask yourself whether losing sleep to read that blog is going further your goals somehow more than if you got the proper amount of sleep.

Addressing "Attitude" Tolerations is more challenging because you must find alternative attitudes that work for you, and you must find alternative behaviors to rely upon when tempted to act in the old way. Just as with achieving our goals, zapping our Tolerations requires Focused Action to succeed.

Attitude or Gratitude? When adversity comes your way, what do you think? "Oh, great, what next? How is this going to affect me?" or "How do I tackle this challenge and solve this problem?" Our attitude affects our outlook, our ability to deal with challenges, and our capacity to master fear. We live in either faith or fear at any given moment. Our positive or negative attitude reflects this.

If you are dealing with fear, how can you change the dynamic and choose faith over fear? Famed psychiatrist and Holocaust survivor Viktor Frankl said:

> *"Between stimulus and response there is a space. In that space is our power to choose our response. In our response lies our growth and our freedom."*

We have the power to choose our response. We can choose faith. As when dealing with "Attitude" Tolerations, you must adopt new habits if you want to sustain your faith. The best way I know to focus on faith is to adopt the habit of gratitude. In the musical *White Christmas*, Bing Crosby croons, "When you're worried and you can't sleep, just count your blessings instead of sheep and you'll fall asleep counting your blessings."

I don't know about you, but counting sheep never worked for me. However, there is a case for counting blessings. Dr. Robert A. Emmons of the University of California, Davis, conducted research into gratitude and discovered those who kept a gratitude list were more positive and also more likely to be making progress on their personal goals.

I believe that there is a distinction between thankfulness and gratitude. To me, thankfulness is a passive activity while gratitude is active. Thinking thankful thoughts is passive. Expressing our thankfulness is taking action: it is demonstrating gratitude.

What is gratitude? Gratitude is faith in action. Writing down and reflecting on the good things in your life is humbling. It is can also motivate us to take action—not merely as a reciprocal transaction, but because we want to be generous and a blessing to others.

Looking at the exercises. Most strategies for dealing with fear and procrastination are reactive. However, we can do some proactive things, too. You are going to start by zapping some of your tolerations, and then you will create a gratitude journal.

Exercise: Zapping Tolerations

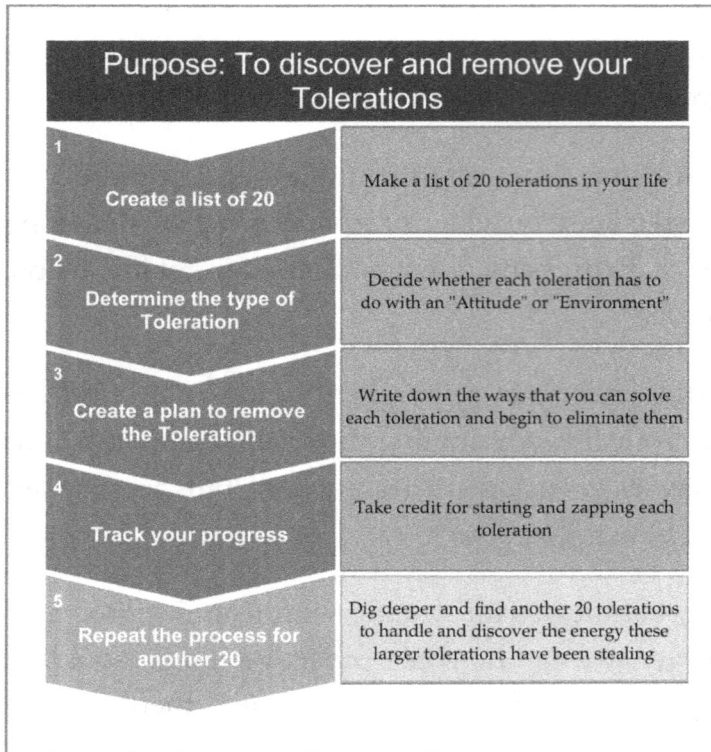

Purpose: To discover and remove your Tolerations	
1 Create a list of 20	Make a list of 20 tolerations in your life
2 Determine the type of Toleration	Decide whether each toleration has to do with an "Attitude" or "Environment"
3 Create a plan to remove the Toleration	Write down the ways that you can solve each toleration and begin to eliminate them
4 Track your progress	Take credit for starting and zapping each toleration
5 Repeat the process for another 20	Dig deeper and find another 20 tolerations to handle and discover the energy these larger tolerations have been stealing

Are you ready to do some mental and emotional house cleaning so that you will have more energy and enthusiasm with which to tackle your goals and ambitions? This exercise has five steps that break into two phases, shown in the graphic.

1. Create a List of 20. Using the worksheet on page 23, list 20 things you are tolerating. Remember, Tolerations are anything you endure in order to get other things done, but rob your energy. They could be small things, such as your messy desk. They might be larger things, like unproductive relationships or pet peeves.

The worksheet has five columns. After the numbered column, each corresponds to a step in the process:

- A handy number to track the Tolerations
- A space to describe the Toleration
- E/A for designating the approach for addressing the Toleration
- A place to describe your solution
- Checkboxes to track progress

At a seminar I gave, a participant told me that he only had three tolerations. When asked if that meant he had no pet peeves or problem clients, he laughed. When he thought about it, he realized that five percent of his clients consumed sixty percent of his time. To add insult to injury, that five percent represented just three percent of his revenue. He realized that he was tolerating some bad customers. By eliminating that toleration and replacing the troubling customers with new ones who appreciated what he could do for them, generated revenues that more than replaced the lost income from the old customers.

2. Determine the type of Toleration. Tolerations are a matter of either your Environment or your Attitude. Understanding which will determine how you handle it. If you do not like where you live, but you have a great job, your toleration could be

- **Environmental:** I need to find a great place to live and change jobs to live a happier life; after all, I can always find another great job.
- **Attitude:** My job is so awesome, but if I didn't live where I do, I wouldn't be blessed with such a great job.

The choice is yours. Do you see how understanding your values can help you decide what is the right course of action for you? The key is to consider which it really is so that you can create a plan accordingly.

3. Create a plan to remove the Toleration. You know what you need to do. Make your plans so you can take action and resolve the Toleration.

4. Track your progress. Did you create a plan? Great! Check the first block in the worksheet. When you complete your plan, Zap that Toleration by checking off the second box. Do you feel the energy surging back into you?

5. Repeat the process for another 20. The second phase is to repeat the first phase, using the worksheet on page 24. I find that for many, handling the first 20 creates space for them to become more aware of the really big things that they are tolerating in their life—sometimes things so big that they do not recognize them as problems. Sometimes you get lucky, like my seminar participant, and discover a big toleration in the first 20, but why not take the time to really discover and eliminate the problem areas in your life?

Why not return to this exercise once a year and see how toleration-free you can make your life?

O: Overcoming You

Zapping Tolerations – First Pass

#	Toleration	E / A	Solution	Plan / Zap
1				☐ ☐
2				☐ ☐
3				☐ ☐
4				☐ ☐
5				☐ ☐
6				☐ ☐
7				☐ ☐
8				☐ ☐
9				☐ ☐
10				☐ ☐
11				☐ ☐
12				☐ ☐
13				☐ ☐
14				☐ ☐
15				☐ ☐
16				☐ ☐
17				☐ ☐
18				☐ ☐
19				☐ ☐
20				☐ ☐

Zapping Tolerations – Second Pass

#	Toleration	E / A	Solution	Plan / Zap
1				☐ ☐
2				☐ ☐
3				☐ ☐
4				☐ ☐
5				☐ ☐
6				☐ ☐
7				☐ ☐
8				☐ ☐
9				☐ ☐
10				☐ ☐
11				☐ ☐
12				☐ ☐
13				☐ ☐
14				☐ ☐
15				☐ ☐
16				☐ ☐
17				☐ ☐
18				☐ ☐
19				☐ ☐
20				☐ ☐

O: Overcoming You

Did you remember to...

- Decide whether each Toleration required a change in environment or attitude?
- Consider your pet peeves?
- Dig deeper by filling in a second batch of 20 tolerations?

Tips for Follow Through

- You do not have to solve all of your tolerations at once. Choose the five tolerations on the list that are bothering you the most and resolve them first. They might not be the biggest changes in your life, but dealing with the things that have the most emotion attached to them will earn back energy quicker.
- You cannot clean a house if you do not see the dirt. You cannot deal with your tolerations if you do not acknowledge them. This is why you need to dig deep and complete the exercise twice.
- Repeat this exercise annually to keep aware of what you can do to continue to get all your needs met.

Exercise: Gratitude Journal

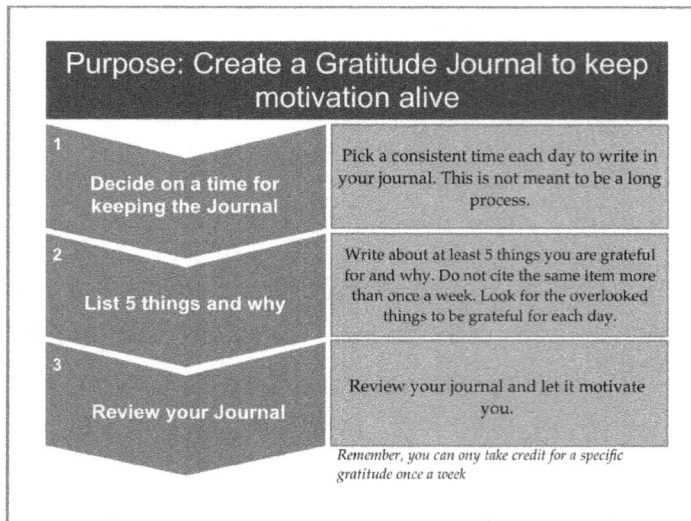

Purpose: Create a Gratitude Journal to keep motivation alive

1 Decide on a time for keeping the Journal — Pick a consistent time each day to write in your journal. This is not meant to be a long process.

2 List 5 things and why — Write about at least 5 things you are grateful for and why. Do not cite the same item more than once a week. Look for the overlooked things to be grateful for each day.

3 Review your Journal — Review your journal and let it motivate you.

Remember, you can only take credit for a specific gratitude once a week

In this exercise, you will keep a gratitude journal for a week. If you start to see the benefit, I hope you will continue to keep a Gratitude Journal. I have prepared two versions of the worksheet. The version on page 28 is a simple list that lets you add as many things as you wish each day. If you are someone who likes a sense of order and doing exactly what is asked, you might prefer the worksheet on page 30, which provides ample space to express gratitude for five items daily. The chart above explains the gratitude process for purposes of our exercise.

1. Decide on a time for keeping the journal. Keeping a gratitude journal is actually relatively simple. However, to get the most from it you must be consistent, so pick a time and stick to it. You might consider journaling when you do the reviews we will discuss in Chapter 4.

2. List 5 things and why. When you think about it, there are many things to be grateful for. For purposes of the exercise, pick at least five people or things for which you are grateful. Yes, some days might be more difficult than others. However, the point of this exercise is to help you become aware of just how blessed you really are. Even on bad days, there are small consolations that can help you keep moving forward.

Of course, you can be grateful for certain things on a daily basis, but if your reason is the same daily, it can only count once a week. The point is to get you to consider additional dimensions of gratitude. For example, I look for reasons to be grateful for my wife Ellen daily. Here is a recent example of how I was grateful for her daily during a week:

- *Sunday:* she planned a great family event we enjoyed with our sons
- *Monday:* she advised me on a business challenge
- *Tuesday:* she works out hard to stay in shape and beautiful
- *Wednesday:* she took care of some business reports
- *Thursday:* we enjoyed time together having frozen yogurt at Menchie's (a frozen yogurt shop)
- *Friday:* she cleaned house, giving us a beautiful place to rest and relax together
- *Saturday:* I was grateful for her example as she shared a lesson from her personal meditation

3. Review your journal. It is fun to think about the reasons you have to be thankful. However, do not let your appreciation for things keep you from taking action in response to these blessings. You are under no obligation to do anything about these blessings, but let them inspire you to do something in appreciation.

When you are discouraged, looking over your Gratitude Journal will also help you see the bigger picture and realize just how blessed you are. And, of course, "When you're worried, and you can't sleep, [you can] count your blessings instead of sheep and [you *will*] fall asleep, counting your blessings."

5 Secrets of Goal Setting Workbook

Gratitude Journal – Week of _____

Date	I am grateful for...	Because...

O: Overcoming You

Date	I am grateful for...	Because...

5 Secrets of Goal Setting Workbook

Gratitude Journal – Week of _____

Sunday	1
	2
	3
	4
	5
Monday	1
	2
	3
	4
	5
Tuesday	1
	2
	3
	4
	5
Thought of the Week	

O: Overcoming You

	Wednesday
1	
2	
3	
4	
5	

	Thursday
1	
2	
3	
4	
5	

	Friday
1	
2	
3	
4	
5	

	Saturday
1	
2	
3	
4	
5	

Did you remember to...

- Put down at least 5 things each day?
    - Where the same thing appears on different days, did you find a new aspect to be grateful for?
- State why you were grateful for things?
- Review your journal?

Tips for Follow Through

- Find ways to express your gratitude for the things you record.
    - Where there is a specific person or organization to whom you are grateful, let them know.
    - Where you cannot express your gratitude to the person directly, the best way to express it may be to share what you gained with someone else: Teaching others what you learned, sharing the benefits of skills you gained, or making a donation in their honor.
- Review your gratitude journal periodically.
    - At the very least, set aside a little bit of time each week to review it and reflect.
    - When you are feeling defeated and depressed is a good time to review and count your blessings.

Chapter 3

A: Achieving Alignment

I would rather be ashes than dust!

I would rather that my spark should burn out in a brilliant blaze than it should be stifled by dry-rot.

I would rather be a superb meteor, every atom of me in magnificent glow, than a sleepy and permanent planet.

The function of man is to live, not to exist.

I shall not waste my days trying to prolong them.

I shall use my time.

—Jack London

Overview of Achieving Alignment

Are you ambitious? What values govern your life? The first two chapters of the workbook focused on how to create a goal and deal with the challenges that can keep you from achieving it. But there are other enemies to achieving your goals. While many are frustrated because they do not have a clear goal to pursue, those with goals can be frustrated if they do not have a clear direction, or burning ambition, to focus their energies. How you pursue your ambition is an expression of your value system (or "values" for short).

There is so much to do, and so little time to do it in. With so many things that we could be doing, how do we choose? Let me ask you, what is really important to you?

Our challenge is we have too many choices. We have many things we would like to do, and many more things others would have us do. Everyone and everything seems to be a priority. So how should we define and shape our priorities?

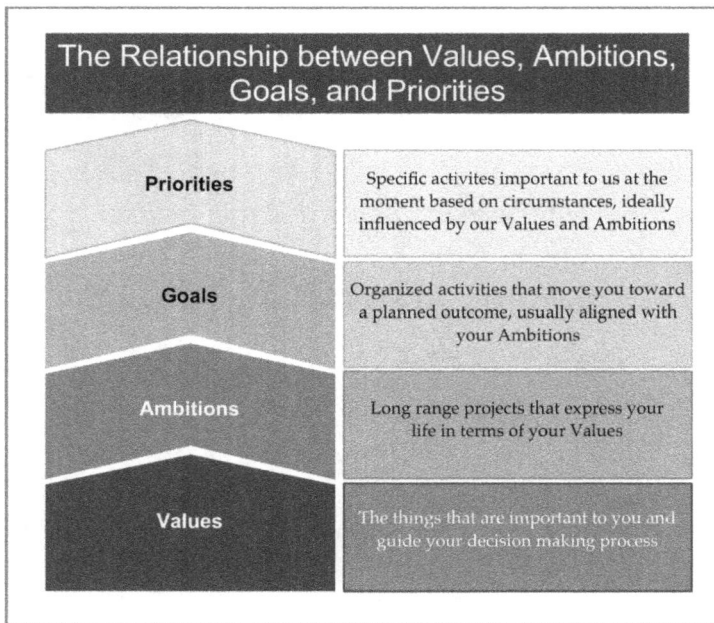

The Relationship between Values, Ambitions, Goals, and Priorities

Priorities	Specific activites important to us at the moment based on circumstances, ideally influenced by our Values and Ambitions
Goals	Organized activities that move you toward a planned outcome, usually aligned with your Ambitions
Ambitions	Long range projects that express your life in terms of your Values
Values	The things that are important to you and guide your decision making process

If you want to live the happiest, most meaningful life you can, you have to consider what you truly value and build your life around those things. The graphic shows the relationship between Values, Ambitions, Goals, and Priorities. The challenge most people face is that they are operating only at the top one or two levels.

If you think of your agenda, the activities you do each day, as a bridge between your past and future, you will understand how important it is to create a bridge that will handle the traffic. Our values are the bedrock upon which we build our bridge. Our ambitions are the posts and footings, driven deep into the earth to reach the bedrock so that the bridge will not move in storms. Our goals are the bridge itself. Clear goals developed with a burning desire have the ability to transport us far. Priorities are the traffic on the bridge.

When we act only on things as they come—without regard to goals, ambitions, and values—we do not have a bridge at all. We are stuck looking for shallow crossings that can accommodate us. Alternatively, we look to use someone else's bridge, possibly paying a toll to use it. People who only ever use other's bridges are often are unhappy with their destination. You must invest in a bridge, either building your own or helping to build another's, if you want to have any satisfaction and success in life. If you are going to invest in another's bridge, however, be sure that you drive your own pilings (ambition) into bedrock (your values) so that your investment will be safe in a storm.

Working with Values and Ambitions. In his speech "Acres of Diamonds," Russell Conwell, founder of Temple University, shared that great riches exist in the things we already have. We have to discover those riches and make them our own. Discovering our values and defining our ambitions unlocks for us the riches in our lives.

How do you consciously decide which of the myriad principles, beliefs, people, or things that you value should receive permission to rule your life? I believe the universe operates with established laws, and that there is objective truth. I teach my clients that when we understand and embrace these laws we can mold the universe to create what we want. Fighting these laws makes success difficult, or even impossible. As Conwell suggests in "Acres of Diamonds," we have to discover these truths inside ourselves in order to use them. Your understanding of these truths may evolve with time, just as your understanding of mathematics evolved from arithmetic to algebra and beyond. Math did not change, you did.

When considering your values, you should reflect on what is important to *you*. Also consider what is true, right, and just. Your intuition knows what is right and what is right for you now. You can ignore the sensation, but you experience it all the same. Trust your intuition.

Ambitions are expressions of aspirations we want to address in our lives. They are the long-term, even life-long, ideas or goals we are chasing. They take into account our skills, knowledge, experiences, and desire. Of these, the last, desire, is most important. Ambition without a burning desire is a daydream. People with significant accomplishments get beyond satisfying their every immediate desire and focus on what they really want. Often, immediate desires are distractions that cause people to focus inward on lower order needs without consideration for their ambitions.

Daily distractions and challenges to our value systems can seem difficult to overcome if you have just begun to clarify your values and ambitions. This is why you need to read your goals daily, and conduct regular review, which will be discussed in the next chapter.

Are you ready to get clear about your values? Your ambitions? The two exercises in this chapter will start you on the journey to clearly articulating both. The first exercise will help you identify which of your core values are most important to you. The second exercise will help you identify and clarify your ambitions. You can also find the worksheet at the end of the chapter.

A: Achieving Alignment

Exercise: Establishing Your Core Values

Have you ever thought about your value system? Do you know which values are most important to you? If not, let's get started. If you have, congratulations! You are on your way to navigating toward your ambitions. You might want to complete the exercise to confirm your thinking, or simply use the form to record the ones that are most important to you. If you have not thought about your values before, you are in for a treat. When you are clear about your values and focus on them as you make decisions, you will begin to get powerful results.

This exercise uses a three-step process to develop your goals, as shown in the graphic. I recommend that you work quickly to complete the exercise. You will use the output to help you with the exercise on ambitions, which will help you deter-

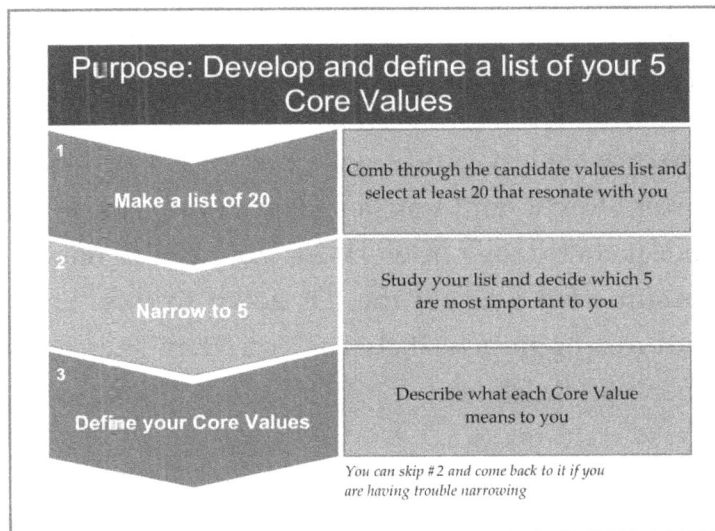

Purpose: Develop and define a list of your 5 Core Values

1 Make a list of 20	Comb through the candidate values list and select at least 20 that resonate with you
2 Narrow to 5	Study your list and decide which 5 are most important to you
3 Define your Core Values	Describe what each Core Value means to you

You can skip #2 and come back to it if you are having trouble narrowing

mine if you have targeted the right core values. Review the exercise in a week to see how you feel about it—perhaps redoing the exercise after you have given your subconscious mind a chance to work on the challenge. Let's get started.

1. Candidate List of Values. Start with the worksheet on page 40. It identifies over 150 candidate values. Most are single words. They should stimulate your thinking. I am not saying that your values should be single words (or that any of these words are your values). While you might settle on a longer phrase, being able to use a single word to describe your values is handy. West Point's values, Duty, Honor, Country, clearly indicate the character of that institution.

Take a few minutes to read the list. Circle or highlight ones that appeal to you. If you do not see something there you think is a candidate value, jot it down at the bottom of page 41 or in the margins. Your goal is to identify at least 20 things that represent principles, ideas, people, and/or things you value in your life.

Work quickly. You will probably find many things that you value. Only pick those that really jump out at you as something about which you feel strongly. Your ultimate goal is to find the MOST important ones for you, so start narrowing now.

2. Narrow the List. Study your first pass list. Pick the five values most important to you and transfer them to the table on page 39. Trust your intuition. If that does not work for you, prune ones you know are not as important until you get the list down to five. Some of my clients struggle with this approach. If that is you, then skip to step 3, and try this again when you finish it.

3. Describe Your Core Values. Now describe what each of the selected values means to you. The words or phrases you chose could mean just about anything to anybody, but they mean something specific to you. Write out these meanings.

Personally, I like short, simple core value lists because they are easy to remember. I like to think of the descriptions as the definitions of the values. The descriptions are useful when sharing values with others, especially when you are working on projects together.

If you find it hard to narrow your list to your most important values before writing the descriptions, just go ahead and write our meanings for all the values you think are important to you. Ultimately, I encourage clients to develop a list of important values that expands the core values to a list of 10 to 20. Creating descriptions for all of your candidate core values can help you clarify all of your most important values.

State Your Core Values

- First, use the worksheet on the next two pages to identify your 5 most important values.
- In the table below, write down your five most important values and then state what they mean to you

Value	Description

5 Secrets of Goal Setting Workbook

Establishing Your Core Values

- Pick 20 candidate values from this list, or jot down your own at the end.
- Work quickly. You will know immediately if it is something that is a strong value.
- Narrow the 20 the 5 most important to you and transfer them to the chart on the next page

Abundance	Composure	Expectancy
Acceptance	Confidence	Experiment
Accomplishment	Connection	Explain
Achievement	Contentment	Extravagance
Adaptability	Control	Facilitate
Add value	Coolness	Fame
Advancement	Courage	Family
Affluence	Creativity	Fashion
Alertness	Daring	Ferocity
Anticipation	Deference	Financial independence
Approval	Determination	Flexibility
Assurance	Diligence	Fluency
Audacity	Discernment	Foster
Awe	Discretion	Freedom
Being the best	Dreaming	Friendship
Bliss	Dynamism	Gallantry
Brilliance	Economy	Gentility
Calmness	Education	Grant
Capability	Elation	Gregariousness
Celebrity	Empathize	Happiness
Change	Encourage	Heart
Cheerfulness	Endow	Hedonism
Cleverness	Energy	Holiness
Comfort	Enlist	Honor
Compassion	Environmentalism	Hospitality
Community	Excellence	Hygiene

A: Achieving Alignment

Impartiality

Individuality

Inform

Insightfulness

Instruct

Intelligence

Intrepidness

Intuitiveness

Involvement

Justice

Leadership

Lightness

Love

Marriage

Mastery

Meekness

Mental

Mindfulness

Modesty

Moral

Mysteriousness

Nonconformity

Open-mindedness

Organization

Outrageousness

Patience

Perfection

Philanthropy

Physical

Pleasure

Potency

Precision

Preparedness

Pride

Proactivity

Provide

Purity

Rationality

Recreation

Relaxation

Resilience

Respect

Reverence

Rules

Sacrifice

Score

See

Self-respect

Sensitivity

Sensuality

Service

Silence

Sincerity

Solitude

Spark

Spirit

Sports

Status

Stimulate

Structure

Supremacy

Synergy

Temperance

Thoroughness

Thrill

Touch

Triumph

Truth

Uniqueness

Valor

Virtue

Vision

Volunteering

Willingness

World Peace

Youthfulness

Zeal

Space for your own ideas

Did you remember to...

- Move briskly through the word list when making your selections?
  - What comes naturally and without hesitation is often most accurate.
- Filter your larger list down to the five that are most important to you?
  - Creating focus makes it easier to act.
  - The smaller the pool of stated values, the less likely they are to be in conflict with each other
  - Many times a broad collection of related values can be best stated under a single heading.
    - For example, if "fun", "excitement", "daring", and "curiosity" are all important ones on your short list, but you don't want to take off "family" or "financial security" to keep all of them, then perhaps you could combine the four under the heading of "adventure", leaving room for your other two values, as well as two additional ones.
- Add your own ideas to the list?
- Make the choices your own by describing them?

Tips for Follow Through

- Understanding your values and the role they play in your decision making process is the key to creating alignment between your ambitions and goals. Take time to "live" with the core values you chose and modify them if needed.
- You actually have more than five values. Consider what other values are important to you. Write them down and describe them, too. Just as with your Goals and Priorities, time and circumstances may change what you most value at any given time.
  - Your principal values are like the stars—they do not change, but which you need to use to navigate may change, depending on where you want to go.

Exercise: Declaring Your Ambitions

What are the big things you want to do? Are they important to you?

Our Core Values focus on the types of things that are important to us. Ambitions are programs we pursue to live our values to their fullest. This means that our ambitions should align with our values.

Have you ever thought about what your ambitions are? If not, this exercise will help you declare your ambition by understanding how the goals you are currently pursuing suggest something larger than those goals themselves. The graphic illustrates the steps.

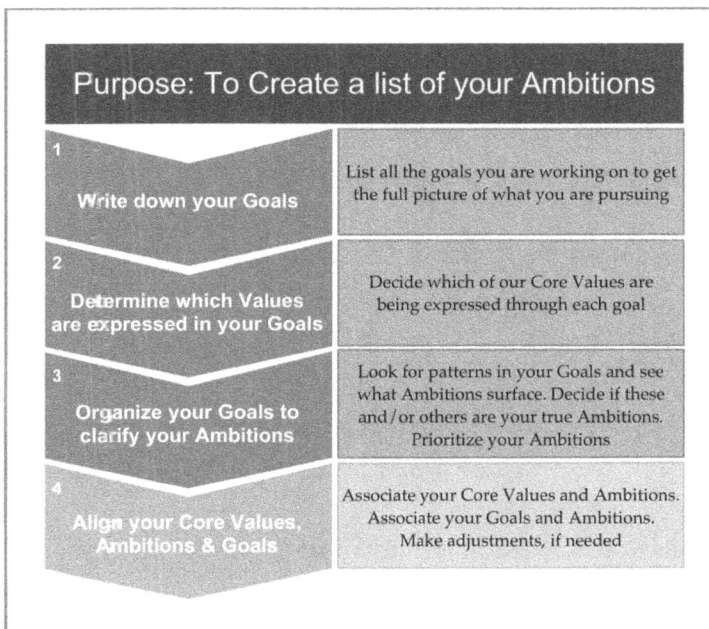

Purpose: To Create a list of your Ambitions

1 Write down your Goals	List all the goals you are working on to get the full picture of what you are pursuing
2 Determine which Values are expressed in your Goals	Decide which of our Core Values are being expressed through each goal
3 Organize your Goals to clarify your Ambitions	Look for patterns in your Goals and see what Ambitions surface. Decide if these and / or others are your true Ambitions. Prioritize your Ambitions
4 Align your Core Values, Ambitions & Goals	Associate your Core Values and Ambitions. Associate your Goals and Ambitions. Make adjustments, if needed

1. Write Down Your Goals. If you are reading this book, I would guess that you are a person who wants to get important things done. That means that you already have some goals you want to accomplish. In the table on page 47, write down all of the goals you are working on right now, or plan to begin in the near future. (Have you developed Goal worksheets for each? If not, why not go back to the exercise in Chapter 1 and complete one for each?)

2. Determine Which Values Are Expressed in Each Goal. Take a moment and think about your goals and your Core Values. For each goal:

- How do your Core Values guide you in its pursuit?
- Which values expressed in each goal?

Jot the core values down next to each goal they influence.

What if you have goals that are not associated with your core values? For the moment, continue to the next step. We will explore this issue a little later in the process.

3. Organize Your Goals to Clarify Your Ambitions. If you want to be a high achiever you have to focus intensely on your ambitions. Begin by studying your goal list.

- Are there long-term goals that fully express your values?
- Are there themes that run through your goal list?

These are candidate ambitions for your life. Consider how your goals work together and identify two to five major ambitions for you to focus on over the next one to five years. Write them in the table on page 49. The larger and longer range your ambitions, the fewer you should have in order to keep focused on them. Here is an example: Say that your goals are:

- Climb the highest peak on each continent
- Write a book about climbing Mt. Everest
- Open a school for mountain climbing

Your ambition might be to be a world-class mountain climber. Or it could be to become one of the world's leading authorities on mountain climbing. How might you tell the difference? Opening the school and writing the book might be goals to help you raise money for your activities. However, if one of your Core Values is teaching others about the majesty of the mountains, then perhaps you really want to be an authority. Neither choice is better or worse, except in how it relates to your values.

Finish writing out your ambitions on the second table and associate your

A: Achieving Alignment

Core Values with your ambitions. Now study the list carefully. Which of your ambitions is most important to you? Go ahead and assign a rank order to your ambitions.

Why do you need a rank order the most important things for you to be working on? When you understand which ambitions have a higher priority, you can see where one ambition is becoming a distraction for another and adjust your activities accordingly. If you find that your circumstances have changed the ranking among your ambitions, you are free to change them and readjust your activities.

4. Align your Ambitions, Values, and Goals. Go back to your goal list and associate your goals with your ambitions, if you can. Naturally, because of the way we did this exercise, some of your goals might be ambitions unto themselves. Remove them from the goal list. Look at the rest. Do they align with your ambitions? If they do, assign the applicable ambition's ranking in the third column.

Study the goals that do not support any ambition. Ask yourself why did you set those goals? Do they really connect to a current ambition, or are they something to defer until other things are accomplished?

Look closely at your goals and ambitions and consider your values. If you have properly selected your core values and ambitions, each priority should have one or more Core Values associated with it. Goals that are associated with an ambition can be associated with that ambition's values, even if the goal does not relate to a Core Value. Sometimes we have to do things that in themselves might not seem important, but are important to larger things.

If on the other hand, you have ambitions or unassociated goals that do not link to Core Values, it should be a warning flag to you. If this is your first time doing this exercise, it could mean that you have not correctly identified your Core Values. It could also mean that the goal or ambition is not as important to you as you think. Consider what you should do. Maybe you need to reconsider your values. Maybe you need to delegate a goal or defer an ambition. The choice is yours.

When you finish, you will have a list of goals and priorities you can be confident will help you express your values and achieve your dreams.

A: Achieving Alignment

Declare Your Ambitions

Linking Goals and Values

- In the table below, write down your major goals in the first column
- In the second column, list the core value(s) that relate to your goal
- After completing the exercise for the table on page 48, return to this table and put the number of the priority that links to each goal.

Goal	Values	Ambition

5 Secrets of Goal Setting Workbook

Defining Your Ambitions

- Study the goals you wrote down on the previous chart. Do some of them connect with other goals? Do they suggest a larger ambition?
- In the table below, write down your ambitions
- Next to each ambition, list the core values it expresses
- Rank each ambition in order, listing the ranking in the third column. Use this number to link each goal in the previous table to your ambitions. If a goal does not link, consider deferring or delegating it. Write a D in the Priority column in that case.

Ambition	Values	Ranking

A: Achieving Alignment

Did you remember to...

- List all of your major goals in the first table?
- Consider all of your core values identified in the previous activity?
- Determine the broader picture suggested by your goals?
- Limit your active ambitions to just a few (two to five)?
- Connect your goals in the first table with the ambitions identified in the second?
- Examine goals that are not connected to an ambition?
  - Consider whether you really want to pursue them.
  - Did you set them or did someone set them for you?
- Examine ambitions not connected to any values?
  - Consider whether you have properly defined your core values and ambitions.
  - If your core values are correct, then it might suggest that now is not the time to pursue that particular ambition.

Tips for Follow Through

- Look at any goals that are not connected to any values or ambitions. Did you set these goals for yourself, or did someone else set them for you?
- Look at any values not tied to at least one of your goals or ambitions. Did you choose these values, or did someone else set them for you?
- Limit your ambitions to just a few things you are actively pursuing. Focus on the ones most important to you. You can change priorities as circumstances dictate. Remember that your ambitions can have stages and that different things can be emphasized in each.
- Create a general plan for each active ambition so that you can focus your efforts in the most effective fashion

Chapter 4

L: Learning and Adjusting

"Your success is based upon your daily habits and agenda."
—*John C. Maxwell*

Overview of Learning and Adjusting

Many people are willing to work hard to achieve their goals. However, people are much more interested in working hard than checking to see if they are really making progress. Perhaps they have heard stories of athletes looking over their shoulders just as they are reaching the finish line and losing to others still looking ahead. Was "review" really the problem? These athletes made two mistakes. First, they were reviewing at an inappropriate time. Second, they were checking the progress of others instead of focusing on their own. These athletes wanted to succeed. What they needed to do was find the right time and the right things to review.

We learned in Chapter 1 that one attribute of a good goal is that it is measurable. If you do not bother to take time to measure your progress periodically, it could actually cost you time in the end. Review allows us to learn and adjust our plans to fit better our situation, our experience, and our needs. Through review, we can see patterns that could be slowing us down and correct them. We might also see patterns that could allow us to double or triple our productivity while saving time and energy. Review also provides us with ideas and techniques we can use in later projects, allowing us to achieve our ambitions in better, more fulfilling ways than we could have imagined when we embraced them.

Reviewing is the intentional act of looking back on recent activities and compare them to our plans so that we can measure their effectiveness and our progress. We need to know what progress we are making. We also need to take a moment and identify potential risks and opportunities. Review helps us maintain focus on the things that are actually important, ensuring that we are getting the job done.

Socrates told his students "the greatest good of a man is daily to converse about virtue." By virtue, he is talking about the things that are valuable and important to us. We want to constantly study the things that are important. If we are not examining them, then life becomes very shallow. For, as Socrates also said, "the unexamined life is not worth living."

Roadblocks to Review. If review is so important, why do people not do more of it? The two biggest barriers to regular review are setting unrealistic goals and our innate human aversion to being evaluated. Before I understood how to set good goals, I avoided reviewing. Half the time I was setting unrealistic goals and then criticizing myself for not achieving them. I found myself spending more time wondering what is wrong with me, rather than resetting a more realistic goal. That's what we do—looking inward and criticizing ourselves, instead of focusing on the problem at hand. Achieving a goal is a long-term endeavor. Not everything you plan for your goals will work the way you expect. If you are taking action toward your goals, mistakes and failures along the way are necessary so that you can find the true path forward.

L: Learning and Adjusting

The third major barrier to review is over-reviewing. Often when people start regular reviews, they spend more time than they need reviewing. Based on your goals, you need to determine how much and how often you should review. In my first adventures in reviewing, I would spend one to two hours daily reviewing. This was much more time than was needed for daily review. Soon, I started procrastinating because I was not getting enough value from all of that review.

Eventually, I returned to reviewing after I discovered that there is a balance and a rhythm to reviewing. While you should review daily, there are other cycles, too. Today, I teach my clients to do four levels of review: daily, weekly, monthly, and annually. The exercise in this chapter will focus on the first three levels.

Reviewing and Planning. Reviewing is a mirror into our plans. As we approach a mirror, things seem to get larger and immediate. When we look into a mirror, we tend to see the close, immediate things first, but as we gaze longer into the mirror, we begin to pick out the larger objects that are not as close, bringing them into focus.

Review is the inverse of planning. When we plan, we need to start by examining our Values and Ambitions, then creating Goals and Priorities, which control our daily actions. When we review, we need to focus first on the immediate, our daily Priorities to ensure we are focused, but then take time weekly and monthly to consider the larger aspects of our goals (and projects), ambitions, and values.

Are you ready to start reviewing? The exercises below are full of great questions that will help you bring your activities into focus at an appropriate level at an appropriate interval, so that you can make everything effective.

Anatomy of Review. Broken into its parts, a review involves three activities:

- Examining
- Evaluating
- Planning

Examining is the process of studying the use of time and resources in support of the goal. You should look at your appointments, scheduled tasks, unscheduled activities, and unplanned activities. Your goal is to understand what you did and why you did it.

Evaluating is judging the effectiveness of the activities examined. You created ways to measure your goals; in this step you will apply them to see if your results are matching your expectations. During this stage, you will also examine deviations to understand their underlying cause. Evaluation is also a time to capture lessons learned.

Planning is determining what needs to be done now to continue progress toward the goal. In the previous two stages, you considered what had been done, why it was done, and whether it was satisfying your needs. Now you need to decide what you will be doing next. Planning can be as simple as affirming that you will continue according to plan. It can also involve reassessing plans in light of new information, risks, or situations.

ACT-ing on Lessons Learned. It is also important to document lessons learned as you move along. They can save time, effort, and money when correctly understood and implemented. One strategy for documenting lessons learned is a method that John Maxwell calls ACT:

- **Apply:** something new that you could apply to your life
- **Change:** an idea or strategy for doing something differently
- **Teach:** something that would benefit others to know

The first step is to identify possible ACTs. As you review, if you see something you might want to apply to your life, put an "A" next to it. If the thing is something you need to change, then put down a "C". If it is something you could teach others, put a "T."

Sometimes these ACTs will be things critical to the success of your goal. Handle those accordingly. Most things, however, are not urgent. Rather, they are fertile ideas that could be done. Some might be distractions. It is easy to become so enthusiastic about your ACTs that they distract you from your goals. Therefore, simply collect the ACTs and review them monthly. Examine all your As, Cs, and Ts, and pick one of each that you can act on for the next few months. Picking just one in each area keeps you learning and growing, but also keeps you focused. Taking your time and deciding carefully what new ideas you will tackle allows you time to consider which are important to you and align with your current priorities.

Exercise: Creating a Strategy for Reviewing

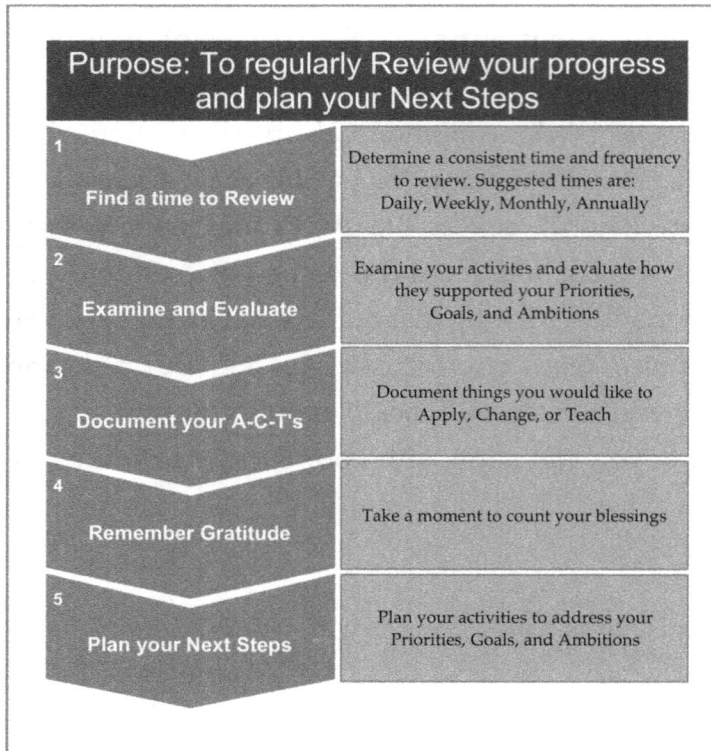

Purpose: To regularly Review your progress and plan your Next Steps

1 Find a time to Review	Determine a consistent time and frequency to review. Suggested times are: Daily, Weekly, Monthly, Annually
2 Examine and Evaluate	Examine your activites and evaluate how they supported your Priorities, Goals, and Ambitions
3 Document your A-C-T's	Document things you would like to Apply, Change, or Teach
4 Remember Gratitude	Take a moment to count your blessings
5 Plan your Next Steps	Plan your activities to address your Priorities, Goals, and Ambitions

Reviews are part of a planning and monitoring cycle; so all reviewing begins by considering the plans you have developed for your goals. Be sure you have completed Goal worksheets for your key goals so that you can keep your goals in front of you. The graphic on the next page depicts a strategy for reviewing.

Before You Begin. You want to be sure you have broken your goals down into enough detail that you can work on them. For many of my clients working on their personal goals, we use a monthly window as the primary timeframe. However, more complex goals might require longer windows. The key is to decide the major things you need do in those timeframes (i.e., each month) to achieve your goals.

1. Find a time to review. With the general plan developed, as you prepare for each month, you want to do your major planning for the month all at once. Usually this means reviewing what you did in the past month, studying what you previously planned to do for the coming month, and decide what you really will do, taking into account circumstances and what you learned from your review. Do not just establish general parameters for the month. Get specific. Decide what should get done each week in the month. If some of the work requires making appointments or scheduling specific work times because of team or resource availability, make plans for specific days.

By doing the major planning for the month in advance, your weekly reviews can focus on progress week to week, and making adjustments to your plans based on circumstances. You will look for trends during the week. This is a great time to evaluate whether you are procrastinating over anything. Use daily reviews to stay focused and committed to your goals. Daily planning focuses on making the next day clear so that you can remain focused on making progress.

2. Examine and Evaluate. The structure for your reviews should focus on the Examining, Evaluating, Planning model, recognizing that Examining and Evaluating are often done in tandem. The questions in the worksheets provide a framework to guide you through the process if you have limited experience. Feel free to expand the questions to meet your needs.

3. Document your A-C-Ts. As the questions suggest, think about the lessons you are learning as you review. Ask yourself if there are things you might want to Apply or Change in your life, or Teach others. Note them so that they do not become a distraction. In your monthly review, consider which A-C-Ts you actually want to implement.

4. Remember Gratitude. A sense of gratitude will help you take action, even when you are feeling stuck. Don't forget to include it as you examine, evaluate, and plan.

5. Plan your next steps. Complete the Examine, Evaluate, Plan process by planning your next steps, consistent with your level of review. This completes the strategy discussed in Step 1. Armed with your plan, continue taking action!

About the Worksheets. If you already have an achievement mindset, you are probably already using some tools to help you manage tasks, appointments, and agendas. I do not want to change how you manage them. Rather, the worksheets provide a way to focus the review activity and to provide a means of documenting review activity. You will find it helpful to be able to look back on the review worksheets to see your thoughts and identify trends you might not see just scanning your diary or productivity tools.

Daily Worksheet (page 60) is checklist oriented and provides a means to see the whole week, helping you to spot trends. You can put checks in the blocks or words, as you choose. There is also a "Thought of the Day" block that allows you to record a daily summary or inspirational thought.

Weekly and Monthly Worksheets (pages 61, 62) are formatted for a free-form response. You can write a narrative covering all the points, number the responses, or totally ignore the questions and write what is on your mind. The choice is yours. The key is that you consider the type things included in the review and document the points.

Annual Review. I mentioned that this is a timeframe for review. What should you do in an annual review? I suggest the following activities:

- Examine your Values
- Examine your Ambitions
- Examine your Goals
- Evaluate your appointments for the year
- Evaluate your use of scheduled and unscheduled time
- Evaluate your A-C-T's
- Evaluate your Gratitude
- Plan for the coming year

Time Required for Reviews. There is no formula to determine the time you should spend on each review. The decision will be based on how you choose to go about planning at the end of the review part of the session. If you are following the process suggested in this chapter, here are some guidelines you may consider:

- **Daily:** 15 minutes
- **Weekly:** 1 to 3 hours, depending on the number of active projects
- **Monthly:** 2 to 4 hours
- **Annual:** 1 to 2 days

Daily Review Worksheet, Week of

Review	Sunday	Monday	Tuesday	Wednesday	Thursday	Friday	Saturday
I thought about my intentions today							
I knew what was important today and I did it							
I was prepared for any appointments today							
I worked on my "to-do's" and not my "to-don't's"							
I used my unscheduled time well today							
What am I grateful for today?							

Planning	Sunday	Monday	Tuesday	Wednesday	Thursday	Friday	Saturday
I have updated plans for tomorrow based on today							
I have planned tomorrow's appointments							
I know which to-do's I will focus on tomorrow							
I have planned for at least one ambition tomorrow							

Thought of the Day

Sunday	
Monday	
Tuesday	
Wednesday	
Thursday	
Friday	
Saturday	

L: Learning and Adjusting

Weekly Review, Week of _____

1. What trends do I see in the preparation, presentation, and outcomes of my appointments?

2. How did my appointments and tasks performed this week support my ambitions?

3. How was my use of unscheduled time? Was I committed to completing planned tasks?

4. What distractions did I allow to take my time this week? What activities triggered those actions? What can I do to control my environment to avoid those distractions?

5. How well did this week's activities support my goals for the month? What adjustments do I need to make?

6. What were my A-C-Ts this week?

7. What am I grateful for this week?

Planning

8. What is the most important task to accomplish next week? Does this support my goals and ambitions?

9. Where can I schedule time to commit to each of my ambitions next week?

10. What does my weekly schedule need to look like next week so that I can make progress toward my goals and ambitions?

Monthly Review, Month of _____

1. What victories did I have this month? Where did I come up short?

2. What is my calendar telling me about my values, my use of time, and my ambitions?

3. How have I been making progress on my goals? My ambitions? Do I need to adjust the plans?

4. Are my goals supporting my ambitions?

5. What new opportunities have come up? Do they support my ambitions? What must I give up to pursue them?

6. How committed am I to my ambitions?

7. What am I grateful for this month?

Planning

8. What do I need to do each week next month to keep on track toward achieving my goals and accomplishing my ambitions?

9. Which A-C-Ts do I want to embrace for the coming month?

10. What other Physical, Mental, Spiritual, Social, and Financial activities should I focus on next month?

L: Learning and Adjusting

Did you remember to...

- Spend the appropriate amount of time on your review?
    - Daily: about 15 minutes
    - Weekly: about 1-3 hours
    - Monthly: about 2-4 hours
- Choose one A, C, and T to work on during your monthly review?

Tips for Follow Through

- Review your daily review sheets during your weekly and monthly reviews.
- You do not have to spend too much time on each review, but spend enough time.
- Consider each active project as you conduct your weekly and monthly reviews.
- Consider the things you are doing that are not part of any goal or ambition. Why are they part of what you are doing?
- In addition to your "to-do" list, consider making a "to-don't" list— a list of things you should avoid spending time doing.

Chapter 5

S: Staying the Course

"I hated every minute of training, but I said, 'Don't quit! Suffer now,
and live the rest of your life as a champion!'"
—Muhammad Ali

Overview of Staying the Course

Setting and achieving goals often works like a trip to Neverland in Peter Pan. We get excited about the prospect that we can fly, and we cannot wait to head out to the second star on the right to find the adventure awaiting underneath. What we do not count on is dealing with the unknown traveling in the dark of night. Challenges and uncertainties can make the night a lonely time. Naturally, once we are at Neverland, there is a whole new set of opportunities and challenges—there are fun things, but there are very real dangers as well. In the end, we leave Neverland because we realize that we can dream bigger dreams and achieve even more in the real world.

We like the idea of achieving our goals and arriving at a destination.

However, the trip itself can get very tedious. Anything worthwhile requires commitment. We do not need commitment when things are fun and exciting. We need it when the long hours of tedium necessary to complete the un-glamorous parts of our goal challenge our will to continue. We do not achieve our goals simply because we start the journey, although it is necessary. We achieve our goals because we take action, follow through, and complete the process.

The biggest challenge to perseverance is discouragement. When you are discouraged, you wonder if you are doing anything valuable. You wonder whether you should continue. Discouragement comes primarily from three sources:

- **Boredom.** Tedium makes people wonder if the reward is worth the effort. This was discussed in Chapter 2.

- **Distractions.** Life gets in the way, sometimes. People can get so busy addressing assorted crises that they lose sight of what they need to do to achieve their goals. They may feel guilty that they have left something incomplete and have not returned to finish it. Often they waste time judging themselves in these situations. Instead, they should focus on re-establishing alignment with their ambitions and start moving again.

- **Inertia.** The tendency for things to continue as they are is inertia. When things are moving smoothly, we do not worry about it because we have momentum. Inertia is working for us. But when things come to a halt because of failure or the unintended consequences of previous actions, inertia is an enemy. It causes people to lose focus, creating confusion and stress.

Boredom and distractions lead to procrastination. We discussed approaches to handling procrastination in Chapter 2. When inertia is working against you, you must get to the heart of the matter and figure out a way forward so that you can keep taking action. The exercise for this chapter will focus on this topic.

Remember to celebrate the victories along the way. Many people that think the only time they can celebrate is when something is completely finished—often calling it "delayed gratification". I support the concept of delayed gratification in its proper context, waiting to get something until you have completed a plan to get it. However, delayed gratification does not mean that you have to give up any possibility of reward or recognition before achieving your ultimate goal.

In fact, failing to recognize the small victories along the way can be counterproductive for you and your team, when pursing a big goal. Celebration does not have to be out of proportion with what has been accomplished, but celebrations are an important opportunity to recognize progress and create excitement for the next phase of the task—especially when you are working with a team. Celebration is a form of gratitude, and can help motivate your team to action.

Exercise: Finding a Way Forward

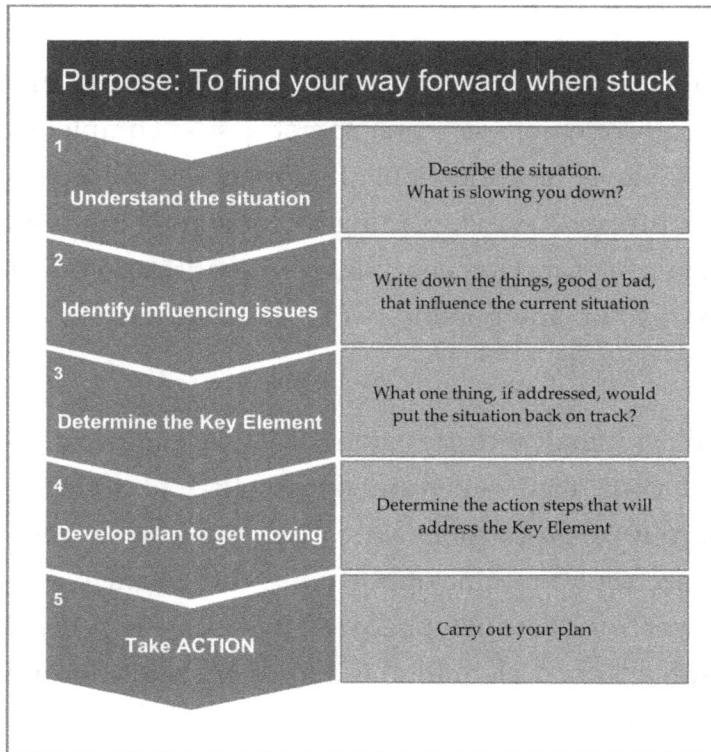

Purpose: To find your way forward when stuck	
1 Understand the situation	Describe the situation. What is slowing you down?
2 Identify influencing issues	Write down the things, good or bad, that influence the current situation
3 Determine the Key Element	What one thing, if addressed, would put the situation back on track?
4 Develop plan to get moving	Determine the action steps that will address the Key Element
5 Take ACTION	Carry out your plan

How do you know that inertia has set in? You are dealing with inertia when you are struggling to move forward, frustrated because you know you are not procrastinating. In physics, force must be used to break inertia. The graphic shows the steps you must take to break inertia. The form on page 70 will help you organize your thoughts.

1. Understand the Situation. In the first block, briefly describe your situation. What is slowing you down?

2. Identify the Influencing Issues. Next, consider what things are influencing the situation. These might be constraints such as budget or regulations, decision makers, the weather, etc., depending upon your situation. Figure out what they are and then ask yourself, "What is the influence?" Is it real or valid? Sometimes we assume things to be limiting our options, but the limit is our assumption, not the thing itself.

3. Determine the Key Element. Now that you understand your situation and the influences, determine the one thing that, if addressed, would put the situation back on track. Notice that I did not say to "solve the problem." Your goal is to get back into action so that you can turn inertia into your friend. Staying still trying to solve the problem does not get you back into action. As you look for the key that would get the situation moving again, you may find the solution to the situation. Great! Treat it as a bonus and get moving!

4. Develop a Plan. Once you understand what will get the situation back on track, determine what action steps are needed. The form has space for four steps, which is often plenty to get into action. If you need a few more, determine them.

5. Take ACTION. Now that you have thought through your challenge and determined a way to start moving forward, take that action and turn inertia into your friend.

Focus on Action

What is the situation?	
What are the influencing or factors, good and bad?	
What is the key element that, if addressed, would put the situation on track?	
List the Action Steps that Focus on addressing the key element	
Action Step 1	
Action Step 2	
Action Step 3	
Action Step 4	

S: Staying the Course

Did you remember to...

- Consider the influencing factors good and bad that contribute to the situation?
- Focus on getting back on track rather than on trying to solve the problem?
- Identify the key element that, if resolved, will put the situation back on track?
- Define clear action steps that will enable you to address the key element?

Tips for Follow Through

- When faced with a challenge, think about what the opportunity is that lies in this problem and you will find new and unexpected ways to achieve your goals.
- Put your plans into action immediately.
- When trying to overcome negative inertia, remember that you do not have to solve the problem that is stopping you. All that is required is that you find a way to start moving forward again. Action and review will yield the solution to the problem.

Next Steps and Support

How to Stay Connected with the 5 Secrets Team

5 Secrets of Goal Setting is an introduction to the whole field of personal development and achievement. I hope that you will continue your journey so that you can have everything you want. To help you, I encourage you to continue your progress. I have some resources that can help you:

- **Read the book.** Have you read the book *5 Secrets of Goal Setting*? Go to http://www.5SecretsOfGoalSetting.com/GetBook for information on distribution.
- **5SecretsOfGoalSetting.com.** The website is a great place to keep up to date with the 5 Secrets community. Our blog will provide weekly tips and stories relating to the GOALS methodology. You can also go there to download worksheets and register for events.
- **Webinars.** Are you interested in learning to apply the suggestions from 5 Secrets of Goal Setting? I will be offering periodic webinars about putting the 5 Secrets to work. The first two will be January 14, 2014. Check the website for details and additional dates.

Do you have a success story about using the 5 Secrets of Goal Setting? Please send me a note at success@5SecretsOfGoalSetting.com. I might even share it on the blog to inspire others.

For 5 Secrets of Goal Setting Workbook Users

5 Secrets of Goal Setting Book and eBook

If you have enjoyed the *5 Secrets of Goal Setting Workbook*, why not read the book and get the whole story?

People wonder, "What secret sets apart achievers?" FOCUSED ACTION is the key to accomplishing your goals and dreams. *5 Secrets of Goal Setting* provides proven strategies that will give you the edge needed to clarify and focus your goals so that you can achieve them, and provides the tools you will need to address the roadblocks and distractions that crop up as you pursue your dreams. Using the GOALS formula, *5 Secrets of Goal Setting* will help you:

G: Get Great Goals – Create goals and a burning desire to achieve
O: Overcome Yourself – Tame the two-headed monster Fear and Procrastination
A: Achieve Alignment – Synchronize your values and priorities
L: Learn & Adjust – See where you are headed to avoid problems
S: Stay the Course – Overcome problems that get in the way of success

You want your dreams. Get *5 Secrets of Goal Setting* and become the unstoppable force that will make them come true.

Available in print and Kindle eBook. Get *5 Secrets of Goal Setting* at http://www.5SecretsOfGoalSetting.com/GetBook.

Goal Achievement Boot Camp

Are you looking to take still more action on your goals? Do you want to develop the discipline to be able to know that something will get done once you decide to do it?

Goal Achievement Boot Camp is a four-week program that digs deep into the mechanics of taking action on your goals. Your cadre will meet for 30 minutes daily via teleconference to learn skills and help each other be accountable to follow through on the actions needed to successfully plan and achieve our goals. Topics to be covered include

- Personal Accountability
- Goal Setting
- Focus
- Creativity
- Purpose

- Power of the Mind
- Achievement Mindset
- Reviewing Techniques
- The Power of Today
- Breaking Barriers

How it works: Odd numbered sessions introduce techniques and provide homework. Even numbered sessions focus on questions and accountability. The whole program makes it easy to learn and act on new habits.

Over the course of the program, you will:
- Define, plan, and begin execution on the goals most important to you
- Learn 10 strategies to help you keep focus and follow through with your goals
- Develop confidence that you can achieve even your biggest dreams

Sign up today and develop the discipline you need to achieve more in the next 12 months than you ever have before. Go to either http://5SecretsOfGoalSetting.com/Events or http://dbaptist.com/mastermind for dates and tuition.

Use discount code *5secretsdeal* and receive $100 off tuition (limit 1 discount per tuition).

No Success is Too Small

Are you frustrated and feel as though it does not matter what you do, you will never succeed? Are your goals looming large over you, mocking you so that you feel as though you are a failure, a fraud?

Many people think that they cannot be a success unless they accomplish really big goals. They are taught "delayed gratification" or "self-denial" until they reach those goals. Frustrated, they give up on their goals and indulge themselves in the things they have been denying themselves, feeling guilty and like a failure.

No Success is Too Small by Dwayne and Ellen Baptist provides a fresh perspective on work, ambition, and success. Through stories and exercises, Dwayne and Ellen will show that you are not a failure, and show you how to celebrate your accomplishments big and small. Through stories and exercises, you will be guided through a process to clarify your passions, ambitions, and values so that you can get focused on your most important goal, building in smaller milestones—places to review, reflect, and celebrate the progress.

Using our past successes as inspiration and focusing our passions, values, and skills to do little things every day we can discover our purpose and achieve great things.

No Success is Too Small will be available in print and for Kindle March 1, 2014. Check http://www.kokorozashipress.com/NotTooSmall for purchase and distribution information.

Gratitude Journal

Documenting what you are grateful for unlocks a lot of potential in your life in a number of ways:

- It reminds us of the good things that are happening to us daily
- It helps us to keep perspective when things are not well, and to see a brighter future
- It calls to mind who has helped us along our journey, and that we need to thank them
- It inspires us to act as a response to the graciousness and generosity we received through our blessings

Sprinkled with wit and wisdom our *Gratitude Journal* provides space to document your blessings for a whole year. The Gratitude Journal provides inspiration, exercises, and tips demonstrating the power of gratitude.

The *Gratitude Journal* will be available for sale March 1, 2014. Check http://www.5SecretsOfGoalSetting.com/GetBook for purchase and distribution information.

The Gratitude Journal makes a great gift for springtime occasions, including Easter, Mother's Day, or as a send-off for your favorite graduate.

Together Inspiring Personal Success

Do you have something you want to change or achieve in your life? Maybe you would like to...

- start a business
- find new love
- get a raise
- lose weight
- get your children to behave better
- or something else

No matter what you would like to change or achieve, the secrets to success are the same:

Define. You have to decide exactly what you want and develop a burning desire to have it. Clarity and a burning desire are critical components of goal achievement.

Become. You will have to change to get what you really want. You will have to develop new skills and abilities, expand your circle of acquaintances, and shed limiting behaviors and beliefs so that you can be the person who can accomplish your goals.

Achieve. You must take focused action to get to your goals, but you do not have to act alone. Few achieve great things alone. Star athletes have teammates and coaches to help them, and fans to perform for. Finding people to help and support your Focused Action improves your chance for success.

Together Inspiring Personal Success (TIPS) is a program that brings people together to experience personal growth. TIPS provides a safe environment to establish goals, get equipped, and find support as you take focused action to achieve your goals. Meeting weekly via teleconference, TIPS members participate in a personal development program while also working on their personal goals in a positive environment.

Join TIPS this summer and get:

- Tools to clarify your goals and develop a burning desire to achieve them
- A personal development system to shed the limiting habits and beliefs that are holding you back, and develop the skills and habits you need to succeed
- Accountability to keep you focused and avoid distractions
- A team to inspire you, and maybe even help you achieve your goals

For more information, visit http://www.successtips.me

Putting the 5 Secrets to Work

Are you interested in putting the 5 Secrets to work in your life? Would you like help getting great goals, reviewing or continuing to take Focused Action? Join Dwayne for a regularly scheduled **Free** webinar providing details that will help you understand and apply the 5 Secrets to:

- Clarify your values and ambitions
- Create a burning desire for accomplishing your goals
- Conduct regular reviews that help you adjust your plans and move ahead
- Conquer fear and procrastination
- Continue towards your goals through Focused Action

For more information and to sign up for this free event visit
http://5SecretsOfGoalSetting.com/Resources

www.ingramcontent.com/pod-product-compliance
Lightning Source LLC
Chambersburg PA
CBHW051418200326
41520CB00023B/7274